# CLARITY
## A guide to clear writing
### Second edition

By Stephen Quinn

Second edition.

Published by MOJO Media Insights, Brighton.

Typeset in Century Schoolbook.

Cover and back photographs by Stephen Quinn

Copyright Stephen Quinn 2018, who asserts his moral rights as author.

Note that this book uses English English rather than American English

## Table of contents

| | |
|---|---|
| Chapter 1: Overview | 05 |
| Chapter 2: The writer's tools | 08 |
| Chapter 3: Sentences | 20 |
| Chapter 4: Planning and research | 33 |
| Chapter 5: Ready to write | 47 |
| Chapter 6: Self-editing | 51 |
| Chapter 7: Style | 64 |
| Chapter 8: Ideas | 69 |
| Useful books about writing | 73 |
| Courses and workshops | 74 |
| About the author | 75 |

Dedicated to all my students

# Chapter 1: Overview

IF YOU CAN walk or talk, you have evidence that you can learn to write. That is the simple message of this book: It is possible to learn to write if you *follow* the techniques in this book and are prepared to *practise*.

But you must be prepared to work. As a baby you could neither walk nor talk. But you learned. You persevered. No-one sprang from their pram overnight to become an Olympic sprinter, or highly-paid actor or courtroom lawyer. We all worked hard to learn to walk and talk because we were motivated.

We made funny noises as we struggled to talk. We fell over a lot when we tried to walk. But we persisted and eventually we became good at talking and walking.

You can also learn to write. But you need to work at it. You will make mistakes, just as babies learning to walk fall over. If you persist and practise you will succeed. Even that Olympic sprinter fell lots of times when they first learned to walk. Even that famous courtroom lawyer or actor has been a little tongue-tied at times.

In the next chapter you will learn about the building blocks of writing, the eight parts of speech. I like to use the analogy of LEGO blocks. You start with words, and assemble them like LEGO blocks into sentences. You combine sentences into paragraphs, and then paragraphs into articles.

Chapter 3 tells you about the three main kinds of sentences you can use, and the three occasional sentence forms that offer variation in the way that spices provide a touch of something extra to a meal.

Chapters 4 and 5 focus on how to plan, research and structure your writing, and suggest ways to improve your prose. They also describe special methods for writing that have proved successful in my classes.

Chapter 6 offers techniques for editing your own work. Writing well is a process, and part of the process involves leaving time to edit your initial drafts. Some wise person once said that writing is actually re-writing.

Chapter 7 introduces the concept of style; that is, how to ensure your writing is consistent in its use of tense, numbers, punctuation and a host of other concepts.

We all need ideas to write about. The final chapter suggests ways to generate an ideas file and develop those ideas.

**Importance of relaxation**
It is vital to remain relaxed, because tension kills creativity. How do we remain relaxed in

situations where we have a deadline? Surely this generates tension?

People have discovered various ways to relax, such as deep breathing or meditation or going for a walk or a swim. Each person needs to learn how to relax. Best to avoid artificial methods such as drugs or alcohol.

What if we cannot start a project? Some people complain of writer's block, another term for the fear of the blank screen or page. Relaxation takes our mind off any task that hinders us, to let our subconscious work on the problem while we are doing something else.

What you need to do is start your project. But above all you need to remain calm and relaxed, because the human brain cannot operate properly when we are tense. And you also need to establish the habit of writing, ideally at the same time each day, so your body-mind comes to expect to work at that time.

I hope you enjoy this book. To repeat: you can learn to write well, provided you put in the effort. And once you have achieved your goal you will appreciate the effort was worthwhile, because the ability to write clearly will pay dividends in every aspect of your personal and work life.

# Chapter 2: The writer's tools

WORDS ARE THE writer's basic tools. All the words in the English language – about half a million – can be divided into groups, known as parts of speech. Think of these parts of speech as building blocks. We build sentences with words the way we build things with LEGO blocks. The way we use those words is what distinguishes between poor, ordinary, good or brilliant writing.

Just as LEGO blocks come in a range of colours, so we have a fixed number of parts of speech: eight. It's essential you understand the role of these parts of speech to enable you to write with skill and precision. Words are the building blocks of creativity.

Skill and precision also depend on practice. We can all learn to write well, just as we all learned to walk and talk. But these did not happen overnight. We all learned to walk and to talk through practice and repetition.

Here is a description of the eight parts of speech in English.

**1. Nouns.** These name people and things. They come in four types:
common
proper
abstract
collective

**Common** nouns: As the name suggests, these label every-day things. They are generally written in lower case and you use your senses to appreciate them. They are touchable or visible. You can hear, taste or smell them. Examples include cat, song, pen, perfume, silk, floor and hat.

**Proper** nouns: These are the names society officially gives to things – such as people, cities and titles. We capitalise them when we write them. Examples include Jenny Brown, Paris and Sir as in Sir Walter.

**Abstract** nouns: These are intangibles such as love, respect and justice. You cannot use your senses to detect them. You must think about them to identify them. You cannot touch justice but you can understand what it means. It is an abstract concept in your brain.

**Collective** nouns: These refer to a group of people or things, such as a school of fish or a herd of elephants. It is fun to make up collective nouns because it gives us a chance to be creative, such as saying a "gaggle of journalists" or a "posse of politicians".

**2. Pronouns.** These represent or replace nouns, in the latter case to avoid repetition. They agree with the nouns they represent in gender and number (singular or plural). Pronouns come in various forms. They change depending on whether they are the subject or the object of a sentence (more on this in the next chapter). Here are some of the most common.

*Personal*: these represent people: I, me
*Possessive*: these denote ownership: my (as in my pen), mine, your, her, his, its, our, their
*Interrogative*: used in asking questions: whose (as in whose pen is this?)
*Indefinite*: these do not refer to specific people or things, hence the descriptor which means "not definite". Examples include anybody, none, some, all, both, any, everybody, several
*Relative*: these introduce or connect clauses: who, that, which (as in the hat "that I wore yesterday")

**3. Verbs.** These express action or a state of being. Most verbs suggest movement or state something happening. But others tell us about existence or being. For example, in the sentence "I am alive" the verb "am" conveys a state of being rather than action.

Verbs are also associated with time, action and person. The time and action element is known as **tense**. So we have present, past and future tense, and three basic senses of action: simple, continuing and completed. Here is an example using the verb "to see":

|  | Simple | Continuing | Completed |
|---|---|---|---|
| Present | I see | I am seeing | I have seen |
| Past | I saw | I was seeing | I had seen |
| Future | I shall see | I shall be seeing | I shall have seen |

Most journalism is written in the **simple past** tense because of the nature of reportage. By the time a story appears, whether later today online or on television, or in tomorrow's paper, it must have happened in the past because the journalist needed time to write the story.

Person: With person, grammarians distinguish between the singular and plural forms. Thus we have first, second and third person singular and first, second and third person plural, as shown below:

|          | First | Second      | Third  |
|----------|-------|-------------|--------|
| Singular | I     | you (thou)  | he/she |
| Plural   | we    | you         | they   |

The use of the word "thou" for you (second person singular) is considered archaic and has been replaced by you.

Thus, in the case of the verb "to see", we get the simple present form:
I see    You see    She/he sees
We see    You see    They see

The simple past version is: I saw / You saw / She or he saw / We saw / You saw / They saw

**4. Adjectives.** An adjective describes or modifies a noun or a pronoun. Think of the "ad" in adjective as a way of remembering this concept – the adjective "adds" to the noun. Another way of expressing this idea is to say an adjective modifies a noun or a pronoun, in the sense of changing it. By far the most common adjectives are the definite article (the) and the indefinite articles (a, an). Some grammarians believe these three words are distinct parts of speech and argue that we really have nine parts of speech, instead of the eight I outline here.

Other forms of adjectives include **demonstrative** adjectives (this, that, these, those) which identify a noun (this cheese or those apples). When used without a noun, demonstrative adjectives become pronouns: <u>This</u> is my apple.

**Possessive** adjectives (my, your, our) show ownership (my cheese; our house). Most other adjectives are considered as being absolute (for example: final, perfect) or conveying a sense of degree or grading. **Absolute** adjectives should never acquire any support because they are complete on their own. It is silly to describe something as "very unique" because unique means, well, unique. Similarly, you cannot say something is "rather perfect" or describe someone as "somewhat pregnant". These words are absolute because they stand on their own.

Adjectives of degree can be: **positive** (used as a simple description), **comparative** (used to compare one with another) or **superlative** (used to compare one with two or more others). Thus you would describe today's weather as hot or a single problem as difficult. But if you wanted to distinguish between two things you would use the comparative form. The weather today is hotter than [the weather] yesterday. Or one examination problem is more difficult than another problem.

In the case of three or more things, we use the superlative form. Thus today is the hottest day all year or one of the problems will be the most difficult you have encountered all semester.

One of the most common mistakes with adjectives relates to confusion over former, latter and last. If you are referring to two things, use former for the first and latter for the second. But if you refer to more than two things, use last for the final thing. For example: faith, hope and love are the three eternal truths, and of these the last is the most important.

**Advice from two great writers**
Mark Twain, American author: "When you catch an adjective, kill it!" By this he means if an adjective is merely decoration or padding, delete it. In the sentence Two people won scholarships at my school last year, "two" is a relevant adjective. It gives useful information. But in the sentence Two straight-haired people won scholarships at my school last year, the adjective "straight-haired" contributes nothing worthwhile and should be deleted.

Denis Butler, the first Australian journalist of the year (in 1976) once told me: "The adjective is the enemy of the noun, and the adverb is the enemy of the verb." He meant that weak or inappropriate adjectives actually diminish the nouns or verbs that are trying to help.

**5. Adverbs.** An adverb describes or modifies a verb, adjective or another adverb. Again, think of the "ad" in adverb as a way of remembering this concept — the adverb "adds" to the other words. The majority of adverbs end in "ly".

Here are some examples: He sees clearly (the adverb "clearly" describes or modifies the verb "sees".) He found a newly-minted coin (the adverb "newly" describes or modifies the adjective "minted".) He recites very poorly (the adverb "very" describes or modifies another adverb "poorly".)

Most of the time you can usually find a more powerful verb to avoid using adverbs. Chapter 4 develops this idea.

**6. Prepositions.** A preposition is a linking word – it joins its object with a preceding word or phrase. For example, in the phrase "a herd of elephants" the object is elephants and the preposition "of" links the phrase by telling us what kind of animal is in the herd. In the sentence "We are heading to Sydney" the preposition "to" tells where we are going. Most prepositions are short words. Some examples include of, to, in, on, for, with, by.

**7. Conjunctions.** These are also linking or joining words. They link similar parts of speech.

Thus they can link adjectives: "fit and well" or adverbs: "slowly but surely". They also link sentences: "You may come. Or you may go." And "You may come or you may go."

The most common conjunctions are: and, but, or, nor, yet, however, if, though, although, either, neither. You need to be able to identify conjunctions because when you know what they are you can delete them to improve sentence clarity. That skill is covered in the next chapter.

**8. Interjection.** The final part of speech is called an interjection. It is a short exclamation that suggests a strong emotion such as surprise or joy or excitement. It always has an exclamation point, as in: "Alas! Woe is me." Or "Wow! What a great story."

As a general rule, good writers avoid using interjections. Using exclamation points for emphasis should not be necessary in formal writing such as an essay, though they are very common in less formal writing such as an email to a friend. In formal writing it is the literary equivalent of digging someone in the ribs to emphasise the punch line of your joke.

**A note about verbs**
Think of the verb as the engine of the sentence. A car with an underpowered engine will struggle. A sentence with a weak verb also underperforms. The verbs "to be", "to have" and

"to go" are the weakest in the English language. Avoid these verb forms.

Instead of writing: The politicians will go to a meeting in Paris next week.

Better to write: The politicians will gather in Paris next week.

Instead of writing: The room has seating for 600 people

Better to write: The room seats 600.

Good writers never use the construction "There are/is/were/has been …." to start a sentence. It's the sign of an amateur. A better sentence almost always hides in the original.

Instead of writing: There are seven teachers at the school who hate chocolate because it is too sweet.

Better to write: Seven teachers at the school hate chocolate because it is too sweet.

**A suggestion:** Improve your loo. The main body of the *Concise Oxford Dictionary* runs to slightly more than 1,500 pages. Park a copy in a place of regular resort, like the toilet, and start reading a page a day. Note words that are new to you, or spellings and definitions that surprise you. Start a personal words journal, adding notes about usages that you encounter. Jot down words you find personally helpful. Also note words you find you use badly or employ too often. List some better options.

You'll discover that words are things with a life of their own and a history. They change, they migrate, they pick up new meanings and they shed old ones. They get tired and confused. They keep changing. Mastery of words is a lifelong pursuit because new words are being spawned all the time.

## The seven powers of words

My friend Mike Paterson alerted me to these powers. Most words operate on several levels, and have at least seven values or attributes:
1. a <u>dictionary</u> meaning (known as denotation)
2. an <u>emotional</u> value (connotation, or feelings associated with its meaning)
3. a <u>sound</u> value (what the reader's inner ear hears)
4. a <u>typographical</u> value (its shape on the page)
5. a <u>rhythmic</u> value (as in the musical feel of a word based on its place in a sentence)
6. the power to <u>rhyme</u> (as in the way it sounds like another word)
7. <u>historical</u> associations (some words like "thou" for "you" feel old and show their history)

Good writers invoke all seven powers. An interest in words is fundamental to becoming a good writer. We need to understand literary concepts like onomatopoeia, alliteration, assonance, similes, metaphors and hyperbole. But above all we need to read to experience a wide array of words.

**Words can be fun**
Did you know, for example, that the words manoeuvre and manure are both derived from the Latin phrase manu operare, "to work by hand". And "floccinaucinihilipilification" is the longest word in the *Oxford English Dictionary*. It means "to estimate as worthless".

An apron was originally a napron just as an orange used to be a norange, but the "n" got detached from the original words. The same thing happened to a nadder, to give us the word for a type of snake. The word "cleave" means both "to stick together" and "to sever".

The English alphabet has 26 letters – 21 consonants and five vowels. English has a handful of words without any of the vowels "a, e, i, o, u" such as tryst, gypsy, lymph and rhythm. An idiogamist is a man who can make love only to his wife.

**Appropriate word choice**
The words you choose must be appropriate for the subject you are writing about. In the next chapter we look at building sentences, using these eight parts of speech, and ways you can write clearly and quickly.

The author took this photograph in the lobby of the *Kansas City Star* newspaper. Ernest Hemingway was a reporter there in 1917-18. His advice still applies.

# Chapter 3: Sentences

THE NEXT PART of the LEGO-block process outlined in the previous chapter involves assembling words into sentences.

But first a word about the role of sentences in the early twenty-first century. People lead busy lives and are time poor. Most want to absorb information quickly to save time.

That is why books are shorter than they used to be two centuries ago. Articles in newspapers are generally getting shorter rather than longer. A short sentence is a great aide to clarity and speed of understanding.

What is a sentence? It's group of words that contains one idea. Ideally you should use short sentences most of the time: An average of 12 to 20 words. This gets easy with practice because through intelligent word selection you will not need as many words as you did in the past.

But too many short sentences can be boring. Vary your sentences to avoid monotony and to give rhythm to your prose. Writers essentially use three types of sentence:

1. Simple
2. Compound
3. Complex

Good writers combine these three with three other less-common sentence forms known as periodic, balanced and loose. Let's look at each.

**Simple**
The simple sentence has one subject and one object or predicate (the phrase or clause after the verb). You will learn more about subject and object later in this chapter.

A succession of simple sentences can be powerful: like pounding your fist several times on a table. Here's an example of a series of simple sentences, taken from the *Faber Book of Modern Reportage*.

> A lorry loaded with stones and rocks backed up. It deposited its cargo in a pile. The crowd moved forward. They started pelting the woman. She was a Muslim. Her face was veiled; her mouth gagged. It was difficult to hear her cries.

**Compound**
A compound sentence consists of two simple sentences joined by a conjunction. We learned in the previous chapter that the most common conjunctions or joining words are "and, but, yet". Here's an example of a series of compound sentences, also from the Faber book. I have underlined the conjunctions.

> The Vietnamese were walking in single file <u>but</u> occasionally the track allowed them to proceed in pairs. The young soldier behind moved alongside me <u>and</u> we glanced at each other. He looked like

> a child playing soldiers <u>and</u> his dull green battledress seemed to swamp his body. His helmet was absurdly big <u>and</u> his American carbine was too long <u>and</u> heavy.

Compound sentences generate a mood of evenness and regularity. They are like the rhythm of regular sine curves. But they can be boring if you use too many together.

**Complex**
The complex sentence has one main statement and one or more subordinate clauses that contribute to the main statement. A clause is a group of words that supports a sentence. Here's an example of a complex sentence that continues the story from the Faber book and tells us what happened to the soldiers:

> When the shelling started it seemed like a small volcano had sprung out of the ground and I felt a tremendous shudder — like standing on a conveyor belt — through the soles of my feet. The air around me, which seconds earlier had smelled sweet, had an acrid taste and my lungs felt congested and burning.

One of the beauties of this paragraph is the writer's use of the senses: we can smell and feel as well as see what is happening.

Good writing consists of employing these three types of sentences, plus the occasional use of three other types. By occasional I mean the way you sprinkle pepper or chili sauce on your meal. Less is always best.

1. Periodic
2. Balanced
3. Loose

## Periodic

In a periodic sentence the climax is kept to the end. Here are two examples. The first is an advertising classic, while the other is from the *Faber Book of Modern Reportage*.

> Even at 60 miles an hour the loudest noise in the new Rolls Royce comes from the electric clock.

> Soon a kindly shroud of snow covered the object and only the toe of a boot or an arm frozen to stone could remind you that what was now an elongated white hummock had quite recently been a human being.

## Balanced

Writers usually need to work hard to create these. They are works of deliberate symmetry; hence the name. Note how this description of the boxer Joe Louis in his prime starts and ends with the image of a spring. Again it is from the *Faber Book of Modern Reportage*.

> He was a big lean copper spring, tightened and retightened through weeks of training, until he was one pregnant package of coiled venom.

**Loose**
These flow from fact to fact in almost a conversational sequence. Sometimes they work but too often they don't reach a climax, which can be frustrating to readers. Sometimes you need to be strong and insert a full point to manage them. Here's an example, under the by-line of Kendall Hill in *The Sydney Morning Herald* of 22 July 2000. I will let you judge whether it works.

> Every cycle and rickshaw, every groaning, crunching lorry, every ox cart and cow and donkey and goat and bicycle and scooter and family van and school bus and even, for dramatic effect, a special rickshaw containing two autistic women who scanned the chaos and absorbed the cacophony around them with beatific smiles as they witnessed the cracked and crowded footpaths with their pushing, chattering, haughty hordes of shoppers on market day examining barrows of fruit and chilies and rice and spices and vegetables, running fingers along lengths of silks for saris and cloth for "suiting's and shirtings," haggling over locks and watches and clocks and denim and gold and occasional furniture but all, eerily, somehow simultaneously frozen in a tableau because, as I've said, the street was completely and utterly congested.

**Rhythm in your writing**
You need to create rhythm in your writing. This is gained through varying sentence and paragraph length, plus your choice of words. Adequate and even good writing can be constructed using a formula. I'm not so sure this

is the case with great writing. Some critics say great prose is in one's genes, or natural like the dust on a butterfly's wings. I suggest it is somewhere in the middle.

One of the best things you can do to learn how to write well is to read great writers. Like a subtle form of osmosis, the rhythm and balance in great writing will seep into your writing the way a prune absorbs water when left overnight in a glass of water (that's osmosis).

> To be a good writer, write! To be a great writer read, then write!
> Anonymous

## Lessons from journalism

We can learn much about writing from the world of journalism. Here are some journalistic techniques that will improve your sentence construction.

1. Employ <u>powerful</u> verbs because strong verbs convey action and save words (removing the need for adverbs).

2. Begin sentences with the <u>subject</u> followed by the verb. In this way you make your point early and put the less important elements at the end the sentence.

The second technique also has the advantage of forcing writers to use the <u>active</u> voice. If you use the active form of verbs, the subject performs the action as in: The rat snaffled the cheese. With the passive form the sentence will always be longer: The cheese was snaffled by the rat.

To find the subject of a sentence, identify the verb and then ask who or what is doing the <u>action</u> of that verb. In the example above, who or what did the snaffling? The answer is the rat, so that cuddly creature is the subject.

To work out the object of a sentence, again identify the verb and ask who or what is having the action <u>done</u> to it. Who or what was snaffled? The answer is the cheese, so that is the object of the sentence.

<u>Tip:</u> If you see the preposition "by" near a compound verb (a verb that is more than one word) it indicates the passive voice, as in "was snaffled by" in the rat example.

### An exception
The active voice saves words and is clearer. But sometimes it is fine to use the passive if the subject is a prominent person.

Thus: *The prime minister was squashed by an elephant when he visited the zoo today.*

This is acceptable because the subject, the prime minister, is considered more important or newsworthy than the elephant.

## Visual writing

Aim to write visually. This forces you to be specific. The human mind responds to images, and other sensory experiences.

> Marvin "Tiny" Smyth eased his 300kg body into the witness chair today to argue that obese people should be allowed to frequent nude beaches.

> After a tough day at work, Minty Crunchback, 60, decided to treat her tired feet by bathing them in methylated spirit while she had a cigarette. She may live.

Get the idea? Sentences that use appropriate words simply and concisely, and which contain an appropriate image, can exude power.

## Number of words in a sentence

The former American news agency UPI asked readers how the length of a sentence influenced their perception of how easy a sentence was to read. They found that the <u>number</u> of words was a key factor in terms of ease of understanding.

The examples on this page and next show how the number of words influences comprehension.

8 or under = very easy: American warplanes have bombed Syria.

11 words = easy: American warplanes have launched a series of bombing raids on Syria.

14 words = fairly easy: American warplanes have launched a series of bombing raids on the Syrian capital Damascus.

17 words = about right: American warplanes have launched a series of bombing raids on strategic targets in the Syrian capital Damascus.

21 words = getting difficult: President Trump has ordered American warplanes to launch a series of bombing raids on strategic targets in the Syrian capital Damascus.

25 words = too difficult: The American President Donald Trump has ordered American warplanes to launch a series of bombing raids on nine strategic targets in the Syrian capital Damascus.

30 words or more = very difficult: Fifteen years after President George H Bush ordered US troops into battle against Saddam Hussein's regime in the Gulf War, President Donald Trump has ordered F-18 fighter jets to launch a series of bombing raids on nine strategic targets in the Syrian capital Damascus.

Aim to write sentences that average about 13 to 17 words. An occasional long sentence will add a touch of spice to your short sentences.

The other key factor that determines a reader's understanding is the number of *syllables* in the words you employ. Aim to use words of no more than two syllables, though some proper nouns will contain more.

Instead of saying the movie Philadelphia will terminate at 3pm, say the film Philadelphia will end at 3pm.

Think carefully before using long or unusual words. The key question is whether your reader will understand them. Unusual words could alienate readers if they suspect they may not comprehend them.

Beware of grabbing for a word and getting the wrong one. If in doubt use a dictionary or the thesaurus in your word processor to find a word you are sure of. I love this example from the TV series *Kath and Kim*, when Kim says to her mother Kath: "I just want to be effluent, Mum."

The dictionary defines effluent as "the outflow from sewage during purification". Kim wanted to be affluent – "abounding in means; rich". What a difference one character makes.

**Summary**
Good writing is an art and a craft. It is an art when it's done well, but this requires a lot of craft and work. Writing involves the third and fourth and (sometimes) tenth draft. **Good writing is really re-writing.** The first attempt is seldom good enough. You may not always have the time to do as many drafts as you would

like. But always find time to make sure you rewrite what you've written.

Tip: It helps to read your words aloud. Your inner ear will detect any flaws in rhythm.

William Zinsser, from *On Writing Well*
Writing is hard work. A clear sentence is no accident. Very few sentences come out right the first time, or even the third time. Remember this as a consolation in moments of despair. If you find that writing is hard, it's because it is hard. It's one of the hardest things that people do.

**Exercises**
1. Fire totally destroyed a house in Yourtown last night worth $50 million.
– Which word is redundant?

2. A woman sprinted very quickly from the blazing house fire after checking her children were safe.
– Identify the tautologies

3. Following a call from a neighbour to the fire station there were three fire engines in attendance.
– How could you improve the sentence?

**More exercises**
Improve these sentences.

1. He suffered the loss of his right eye in an accident.
2. They reached a settlement of the debt.

3. Brown, a family man, has a wife and four children.
4. Not until late August did she finally receive the money.
5. Applications must be submitted on or before the deadline date of 1 May 2020.
6. A pay rise of 13 per cent was received by the carpenters.
7. It is estimated by police that the boys drowned at 4.10pm.
8. The politician extended his appreciation to those who had supported him.
9. The blaze initiated at about midnight in the vicinity of the high school's café.
10. The bank loan was made to the couple for purchase of a new home.

**Answers to exercises**

1.1 The verb destroyed includes the concept of total destruction, so we do not need the word "totally".

1.2 Better to say: A woman fled the blazing house after checking her children were safe. The powerful verb "fled" replaces the phrase "sprinted very quickly" and "blazing house fire" becomes "blazing house"

1.3 Better to say: Three fire engines attended after a neighbour called the fire station.

2.1 He lost his right eye in an accident.
2.2 They settled the debt.
2.3 Brown has a wife and four children.
2.4 She did not receive the money until late August.
2.5 Applications must be submitted before the deadline of 1 May 2020.
2.6 The carpenters receive a pay rise of 13 per cent.
2.7 Police estimated the boys drowned at 4.10pm.
2.8 The politician thanked those who had supported him.
2.9 The blaze started about midnight near the high school's café.
2.10 The couple got a loan to buy a new home.

# Chapter 4: Planning and research

PLANNING IS VITAL, and so is research. The trick is doing the best amount in the available time. Avoid getting swamped in detail. If you're writing a 1,000-word feature or essay you do not need to plan as much as for a book chapter. Planning helps you decide what to cover and what to omit.

Here are some questions you need to answer:
- What's the article about? What's the idea that led to it?
- Who are the main people involved?
- What are the main acts or actions that need to be discussed?
- What consequences are likely from those actions?
- What does all this mean for the reader?

The key information building blocks for writing are primary and secondary sources, such as quotes from interviews (primary) and facts from books and web sites (secondary). We are dealing here with writing for print, but it's worth noting that other important ingredients such as photographs or video and audio can be used for broadcast and online composition.

Here are good ways to do research:
- Consult experts
- Interview key people such as eyewitnesses, relatives, friends and opponents

- Check earlier stories on the subject via the web to see what ahs already been written
- Research official records and reports. This includes minutes, speech notes, scientific and learned journals, academic papers, maps, video recordings, diagrams, letters, reference books, almanacs, yearbooks, or collections of statistics
- Visit the scene to absorb the atmosphere and understand the area
- Approach specialists (such as pressure groups, NGOs or lobby groups)

Unless you're an acknowledged expert on the subject, you gain authority by going to authorities. Rarely will one expert be enough. A beef producer might be an authority on his own herd but this does not make him an authority on national beef policy.

**The angle**
Your choice of angle is important. You must decide which approach is current and the most interesting. This means you must read newspapers and magazines and monitor web sites to be up to date on your subject.

A useful way of finding your angle is to consider your material the way a videographer does. When they're shooting a scene they use a wide-angle establishing shot, then a medium shot of the scene to be highlighted, a medium close-up of the key subject and then they zoom in for a close-up. Or they might decide to begin with a close-up and then zoom out to include the whole scene.

Writers have been using this technique long before the movie camera was invented. The trick is deciding what aspects of your material to focus on, always remembering you're looking for the most interesting angle. Sometimes you won't be sure of your angle until you've done a great deal of research.

**Advice about interviews**
Do your homework before interviewing your main source or sources. This means going to the library or finding reference material and experts on the web and in databases. You need to be prepared before you meet the people who will give you vital information.

We continue now with the analogy of writing as a building process using LEGO blocks. The information you gather during research represents more building blocks to help you structure your writing. As with all building projects, hopefully you will use the finest and discard the lesser materials.

Begin by going through your research and interviews and identifying the key facts about the piece you intend to write. It helps to highlight them in your notes and assemble them ready to be used.

Review your interviews and look for the best quotes. Find informative and eloquent answers. Journalists use quotes to add authority to the statements they make in their writing. Quotes also help with the pace of an article, introducing fresh voices to break up the narrative.

Then you need to start organising and prioritising this material. Journalists use a method known as the *inverted pyramid*, and this represents a useful tool for structuring any article. A model is shown on page 41. The best and most substantial information goes at the start of the article and the material then tapers away, with the facts and quotes getting less significant further down the article.

Journalists refer to the *5W+H* to help them remember the important components of any piece of writing: *who, what, when, where, why* and *how*. You should answer most of these questions early in any piece of writing, not just journalism.

The facts need to satisfy those six journalistic watchwords: who, what, when, where, why and how. One way to remember this process is to remember a piece of poetry by Rudyard Kipling. Kipling started as a journalist before he became a novelist. He won the Nobel Prize for Literature in 1907.

"I keep six good serving men
 They serve me well and true.

Their names are what and where and when
And how and why and who."

Unless the piece you are writing satisfies all of the six key elements reasonably quickly, it is inadequate. You do not need to cram all six into the first paragraph. That would be like stuffing your mouth full of food at dinner and then trying to sing. The six elements should be covered in the first three or four paragraphs.

To Kipling's poetry I have added:
"Oops, and I almost forgot
Remember to ask "so what?"

The point of the last two lines is to ensure what you plan to write about is worth bothering with in the first place. Do you have a story to tell?

We next need to consider the opening couple of sentences – known as the introduction. It is the most important part of any piece of writing because it sets the tone of what the reader will encounter. It is vital you make the most of these opening sentences. Journalists call it the "lead" or "lede" (rhymes with speed) and often abbreviate it as the "intro".

Think of it as a shop window where the best goods are displayed to draw readers inside.

**Writing the lead**
Perhaps you will choose to grab readers by the scruff of the neck and demand they read. Or you might aim to startle or entice them with some

tantalising fact, or use a question. Or you might choose to be persuasive and subtle.

The style and tone depends on the type of article you are writing. It would be wrong to suggest a formula for introductions. But these general points are almost universal. Your introduction should:
- be appropriate
- be brief
- compel the reader to continue
- summarise the key point of the article
- satisfy at least a couple of the who, what, when, where, why and how questions.

Let us look at each of these elements in more detail.

**Appropriate:** Set the tone you intend for the article. Serious subjects require serious introductions. Lighter subjects can have funny or light-hearted leads.

**Brief:** A short opening paragraph will always be more attractive to busy people than a mass of text that fills half a page. Use two or three sentences, of about 12-18 words each.

**Compelling:** Most readers are busy people. One of the chief jobs of the introduction is to entice or compel the reader to continue reading despite their being busy.

**Summary:** Base the introduction on the main outcomes of your research. By the end of the first two paragraphs the reader should have a clear idea of what the article is about.

Here is an example from journalism to illustrate the summary concept:

Fire destroyed a restaurant in Yourtown yesterday just before it was due to re-open after £15 million of renovations.

In a few words the opening sentence tells us:
1. Fire destroyed a restaurant that had been renovated (what)
2. The renovations cost £15 million (how much)
3. The fire occurred in Yourtown (where)
4. The fire occurred yesterday (when)

We get several crucial facts in 19 words. And we generate questions in the audience's mind, making them want to read further to get answers to those questions.

These queries might include: Who owned the restaurant? What kind of renovations cost that sort of money? In what street or suburb did the fire occur? What caused the fire?

For the rest of the article, the writer's job is to answer those questions in a logical order. The order depends on the audience. For an audience interested in money, details of the renovations would come next.

**A tip on composing introductions**
Think to yourself: How would I tell this story to my friends when I see them later today for a coffee? The way you would start telling a story verbally is often a good guide to the way you should start telling it in written form.

Why this approach? Because your mind automatically goes to the most interesting or newsworthy aspect of the incident. You might say to your friend: Guess what I learned today. The owners had just spent $15 million upgrading that restaurant but it burned down just as it was about to re-open.

**Guidelines for writing introductions**
Never start with a direct quote (words in quotation marks) because the reader does not know who is speaking.

Avoid starting with a number unless it's the only possible way, and if you do then write the number in full. If it's more than a two-word number, find another way because a large number without context will confuse readers.

Avoid negatives. Find a way to say even a negative in a positive way. We learn more about this in the next chapter.

Avoid inverted sentences. Put the subject first, not the subordinate clause. This was discussed in the previous chapter.

## Constructing the story

Earlier we met a common technique in journalism called the *inverted pyramid*. The most important information is put into the first paragraph, and thereafter the next most important facts go in the next paragraph, and so on to the end. It looks like this:

>       Introduction containing most important
>        and/or most interesting information
>         Development of these main facts;
>            plus supporting quotes
>           Introduction of lesser facts;
>            development of lesser facts
>           Then supporting information
>              or background info
>            Good quotes plus more
>               facts of lesser
>                 importance
>               Minor detail,
>                developed
>                if there's
>                  space
>               The least
>                 signif-
>                  icant
>                  info

This is simply a diagram. This collection of facts, quotes and background information needs something to link one paragraph to the next so the story flows. You, the author, add a thread of continuity.

You do this by using transitions – words that link one paragraph with the next. Examples include however, meanwhile, moreover, but, later and despite, plus intelligent repetition.

**Some tricks with transitions**
It helps to repeat key words to ensure your article flows. In this example, the key words and transitions are underlined:

> Belmont College has established a special committee to discuss what the principal calls an "excessive" number of high distinctions.
>
> Principal John Baqua said three in four students received grades of more than 90 per cent last semester.
>
> But the committee cannot meet until all examination results have been processed.
>
> Meanwhile, a group of senior students plans to organise a protest over the closure of the new sports facilities and the cut in study hours at the library.
>
> Despite the protest plans, Principal Baqua said he would welcome the chance to meet student leaders.

Good writers operate on two levels when constructing an article. They write each sentence bearing in mind its internal structure, and they also consider each sentence's role in the overall structure.

Construction also takes place on two levels: It happens initially when you are collecting information, and later when you write. This process is known as sequencing – finding the best way to tell the story.

As Bob Baker writes in *NewsThinking*: "The chronology must sometimes be discarded and replaced by an outline of facts that emphasise the *essence* of the story." This principle of journalism applies to most forms of clear writing.

**Tricks when constructing a story**
As you write each sentence, ask yourself what questions will arise in the reader's mind as they encounter that sentence. Then answer those questions.

Keep your reader/audience in mind as you write. You know a great deal about the subject, but they know relatively little. You need to consider what they need to know to understand the situation. How much explanation will you need to include? What will be new for them? What will they find interesting? What will grab their attention and hold their interest? Will they be able to follow the story easily?

Think in terms of simplicity and economy of words. Keep sentences short. Be consistent with verb tense. Watch your grammar, spelling and punctuation. Accuracy is vital because errors destroy your credibility.

**A note about accuracy**
Good writing has three levels of correctness:
1. Correct grammar, spelling, usage and style
2. Choice of words appropriate for the audience
3. Accurate in terms of facts

Use the spell-check on the computer but remember that it will only pick up spelling mistakes – it will not tell you if you've written the wrong word or misspelled a name or left out a letter. Here are some examples:

> Child abuse is a treat for small children.
>
> The writer meant: Child abuse is a threat to small children
>
> The former editor of the newspaper, Peter Blunder.
>
> The real name of the former editor of the newspaper is Peter Blunden, so the writer has maligned that former editor.

Use a thesaurus to help find the right word. Online dictionaries are helpful, as is Google's search tool (type "define xxxxx" where "xxxxx" is the word you need to clarify). Online spell checkers such as this one can be useful: http://www.spellcheck.net

Purdue University in Indiana in the United States has an excellent Online Writing Lab (OWL) with factsheets and exercises on grammar, punctuation and spelling. Find it at: http://owl.english.purdue.edu/owl/

**Introduction exercises**
Write an introduction for each of these situations. Write no more than two or three sentences (somewhere between 30 and 50 words). All scenarios are fictitious and were created as learning exercises. Make people want to read your story. Then use bullet points to explain how you would develop and structure the article.

1. Gladys Anne Riggs is 81 years old. Her husband, George, died 10 years ago. She is retired and normally receives about $4000 a month in social welfare benefits. She tells you she has not received her payments for the past four months. When she inquired as to the reasons for the troubles, officials at the Department of Social Welfare (DSW) office today explained that she is dead. A DSW spokesman tells you: "Four months ago, her cheque was returned and marked 'deceased,' so all her benefits were cancelled." Because of the error, Mrs Riggs has no money to buy food and to pay rent. She lives alone in a one-bedroom flat and says she has already fallen behind in her rent and is afraid she will be evicted. Social Welfare officials said that they will correct the problem as soon as possible and that she will

receive a cheque for all the benefits she has missed during the past four months, but that it may take several weeks to issue the cheque.

2. Security personnel at a local Bi-Lo store arrested another shoplifter today. He was observed stealing a $9.98 pair of sports shoes at about 3pm. Mary Chung, who was cleaning one of the aisles, said she saw him put the shoes in a plastic lunch bucket, then leave the store without paying for them. She notified the store's manager, and he apprehended the shoplifter in the store's parking area. The shoplifter did not offer any resistance. He did not even cry. Police were called to the scene and took the shoplifter to a home for delinquent children. Because of the youth's age, they were unable to release his name. He is six years old. The store filed a complaint against the boy. The police charged him with shoplifting and then released him to his parents. Police believe he is the youngest person they have ever arrested.

# Chapter 5: Ready to write

BEGIN BY STATING in one phrase or sentence **what** your story is about. Write it at the top of the page or stick it above your word processor or laptop. Post-it notes are useful here. This will remind you of the focus of your story, and can be helpful if your mind wanders.

Start as soon as you've done your research while your mind is fresh. Procrastination remains the thief of time. The more you dither, the more likely you'll lose your enthusiasm.

It's also helpful to review the questions you began with. Why is this happening? What is the conflict? What does it mean to readers? Remember to ask the questions an intelligent reader would ask. Then make sure you *answer* them.

Strong stories come from the use of powerful verbs and specific nouns. Concentrate on powerful verbs to drive your story. Remember the basic news reportage style of using single, active and declarative (SAD) sentences. Know what to discard and what to keep. This will become more apparent in the editing process (discussed in the next chapter).

Genuine style is not manufactured; it is natural. It reflects the kind of person you are. Style can be worked on and polished but it's not created artificially through the desire to impress. Style is distinguished by clarity and integrity. It evolves, sometimes spontaneously, out of an understanding of the basic principles of writing, research and character (who you are and your experiences of the world).

Here is a technique I have often used that might help those who struggle to start. I call it **"vomit copy"** because the aim is to blurt out your words without thinking, the way your body purges when you are physically sick.

In summary, you:

- Set an alarm for, say, 30 minutes
- Promise yourself you will write nonstop until the alarm goes off
- Cover the screen of your laptop. If writing longhand, do not read what you've written
- Vomit the words onto the screen. If you cannot think of what to write, or your body protests, include those thoughts in your projectile writing. For example, you might write "This is crazy. I feel like a fool doing this. My stomach hurts and I feel silly. I hate this." You can always delete these words later
- Refer to the summary of what your story is about if your mind goes blank
- Remember that writing is really re-writing, so you will edit your words later. For the moment the aim is to blurt

- everything out from your head onto the screen or paper
- Once the alarm sounds, save your file on the word processor and take a break
- Reward yourself for all your hard work
- With practice you can increase the amount of time for this exercise, ideally to a minimum of one hour

## Why this approach?

We have two hemispheres in our thinking brain, or neo-cortex. The left hemisphere is good at criticism and analysis and ideal for editing. But we need words we can edit.

By covering the screen and blurting out those words, you are ignoring your critical left hemisphere and letting your right hemisphere have some fun. That hemisphere is all about rhythm, music and imagination but it tends to be suppressed by the left hemisphere.

Because the screen is covered you will not notice spelling errors or typos. This process briefly silences that voice on your shoulder who criticises everything or wants to fix typos (*"Hey, your grammar is wrong there"*). It allows your natural creativity to flourish.

Most people can type at least 50 words a minute (an option if you type slowly is to use voice recognition software). So if you type or talk nonstop for half an hour this will produce 1,500 words. An hour will get you 3,000 words. Even after you delete the rubbish the words that remain will feel fresh and zesty. And you will notice rhythm and flow to your writing that does not appear when you monitor the screen and correct as you go, or re-read and edit your handwriting after every sentence.

This approach might feel uncomfortable at first and your body might resist. As mentioned earlier, you might develop a headache or discover a desperate need to bathe your dog or clean the windows. You need to promise yourself you will push through these mental objections. One way to deal with these distractions is to write them into your vomit copy – I've got a headache and/or I really need to wash the dog – because you can always delete those words when you edit.

With practice you might find you go to another place during this process, and do not return until you hear the alarm. And you will find, almost like magic, a rainbow of beautiful words on your screen or page (as well as references to bathing the dog). Now it is time to edit those words, the subject of the next chapter.

# Chapter 6: Self-editing

GOOD WRITERS LEARN to edit their own writing. This chapter offers an approach from the world of journalism. But the principles can be applied to most forms of writing.

When self-editing I employ an image of a passkey, the key to success as a writer. Think in terms of ensuring your writing is PASSC:

1. **P**ositive
2. **A**ctive
3. **S**pecific
4. **S**imple
5. **C**oncise

This chapter will look at each of these elements and then offer ways to improve clarity and meaning.

**Positive**

A writer's job is to tell people what has and what is about to happen. With a few exceptions, readers are generally not interested in what has not happened. Sentences should assert.

As a general rule, compose your prose in a positive form. Thus instead of:

> The council says it will not now proceed with the new project.

Better to say:

> The council has abandoned the new project.

Instead of:

> The company decided it would not pay attention to the complaint.

Better to say:

> The company ignored the complaint.

Exceptions apply to every rule. If your local government has decided not to spend £300 million on a new cultural centre, after announcing a year ago that it would, then you may need to say just that.

But you can generally find a way to express most negatives in a positive form.

### Active

Almost all clear and powerful writing employs the active voice. This is where the subject does something, rather than has something done to it. The latter is called passive voice. Active voice is almost always clearer and more concise.

You will encounter passive voice in many official documents. Terms like:

> It was decided that ...

Or

> Under the circumstances it was deemed appropriate that ...

This kind of phrasing often says nothing, which is presumably what some officials are trying to do. It also obscures the meaning: who made the decision in the first example? Who considered it appropriate in the second?

Your job is to write in such a way that the reader knows what is going on. As outlined in chapter 2, one way to do that is to use powerful verbs. Often the verb is hidden in the sentence.

Instead of this verbose statement:

> A gathering of the teachers will be held next week.

Better to begin with the subject:

> The teachers will meet next week.

The second version is clearer and uses fewer words.

## Warning

One of the things you will find when your writing is active and positive will be the need to clarify points of information.

People sometimes use negative phrasing and passive voice when they do not know what they mean or as a way to avoid decisive expression. To write well you need to understand the facts.

Take the example on the first page of this chapter of the council that "says it will not now proceed with the new project". Before you can write it as "has abandoned the new project" you need to know if the company has actually abandoned the project, or whether it is simply delaying it.

Seeking clarification will lead to more information. In the latter case you would need to say the company had postponed the project. Speaking or writing in active verbs calls for the confidence that comes from knowledge.

**Some useful advice**
The passive voice is often the refuge of uncertainty. If I say that creditors are allowed to use force in collecting debts, I do not need to say who or what allows it: the law, local custom, the police, the absence of police; and that enables me to disguise the fact that I don't know, or am not sure, or don't want to say. Which may be convenient, but doesn't make for good, clear writing.
John Whale, from *Put it in Writing*

**Specific**
The writer's job is to find *le mot juste*, as the French say, the right word in the right place. One way to get the right word is to be specific.

Prefer concrete words and avoid vague terms. To return to chapter 2, use concrete nouns. People can relate to things they know. Vague words are unsatisfying as well as unclear.

Fill your prose with detail and facts. Give readers specifics.

If you take care of the individual words, the story (and style) will often look after itself. Every word in your writing must earn its place.

For example:

> The city council has passed a by-law banning families with small children from certain congested parts of town such as Sunshine Plaza.

What are "families with small children? Are we referring to children under eight years of age, or under 100 centimetres (40 inches)? What are "certain parts of town"? Be specific.

Better to say:

> Children aged eight or under have been banned from Sunshine Plaza. The city council last night decided that part of town was too busy for children.

Here are some examples of woolly sentences that can be improved if you are more specific.

> They accepted employment on a part-time basis.

Better to say: They accepted part-time work.

> The tenants were seeking participation in the making of rental price policy.

Better to say: The tenants wanted to help decide the rent.

> The government acknowledged that the teacher supply situation is serious.

Better to say: The government admitted to a scarcity of teachers. Or: Teachers are scarce.

Remember that the verb is the *engine* of the sentence. Your job is to find a powerful verb to drive each sentence.

**Simple**
Writing simply is not writing for an audience with an intellectual age of 12, as some critics of the media have suggested. Simple writing is clear writing. The best writers in the English language in the past two centuries have known that elegance is contained in simplicity. It is the best way to be understood.

A full stop is one of the best ways to simplify a sentence. One **idea** per sentence is a good rule for clear writing. Hence the recommendation to use simple sentences in chapter 3 because a simple sentence contains only one idea.

Sentences should travel without excess baggage. Remember from chapter 2 that the adjective is often the enemy of the noun and the adverb the enemy of the verb. Adverbs and adjectives, unless appropriate, diminish verbs and nouns.

As the great author Mark Twain said: "When you catch an adjective, kill it!"

Good writing contains two types of adjectives and two types of adverb: relevant and irrelevant. If you are describing an accident in which three people died, three is a relevant adjective. It contributes to the story. It tells the reader something useful.

But to say that three flaxen-haired people died in the accident contributes little to the story. And to say the accident happened "suddenly" or "violently" is pointless. Surely all accidents happen suddenly and involve a degree of violence.

**Golden rule:** If something is exciting or funny or shocking, let the reader deduce the facts from the events. Nothing is more absurd than somebody trying to suggest an event is exciting through the use of adverbs and adjectives. Powerful verbs convey this sense more elegantly. Otherwise you end up sounding like a parody of tabloid journalism.

Aim to write with nouns and verbs. Use this formula: **Subject + verb + object**

That is, the subject – usually a noun or pronoun – then a powerful verb and then the result of the action of that verb.

The *Lord's Prayer*, one of the most beautiful pieces of prose ever written, contains only one adjective. (What is it?) *Genesis* did not begin with: "An amazingly exciting account of how one man brilliantly created the whole of the world in the incredibly short time of six days."

## Concise

Using specific and concrete terms is part of being concise. They help you write more sharply. The secret to writing concisely is to choose the shortest and simplest words, and employ the most powerful verbs.

"If I had more time, I would have written a shorter letter." (Mark Twain)

Below are some phrases that are full of circumlocution. Notice how shorter and clearer the terms become when you remove the underlined redundant words:

<u>absolutely</u> perfect        <u>acute</u> crisis
adequate <u>enough</u>          <u>a distance of</u> 12km
<u>a period of</u> time         appear <u>on the scene</u>
<u>all-time</u> record          appointed <u>to the post of</u>
appreciated <u>in value</u>     ascend <u>up</u>
attach <u>together</u>          <u>final</u> destination
<u>awkward</u> predicament      <u>a number of</u> examples
among the delegates <u>expected to attend</u>

In the right-hand column you will find a shorter word or phrase for the words at left.

| | |
|---|---|
| Abrasions and contusions | cuts and bruises |
| Ahead of schedule | early |
| A large proportion of | many |
| Ascertain | find out |
| At an early date | soon |
| At the present time | now |
| Called to a halt | stopped / ended |
| Caused injuries to | injured |
| Continued to remain | remained |

## Write for clarity

Good writers avoid pretension. Some words may sound impressive, but your job is to get your message across clearly and quickly, rather than impress. Here are some pretentious words to avoid. Construct your own list.

| Avoid | when you can say |
|---|---|
| accommodations | rooms |
| annihilate | destroy |
| circumvent | go around |
| endeavour | try |
| expedite | hurry |
| indolent | lazy |
| parsimonious | stingy |
| terminate | end |
| utilize | use |
| vanquish | defeat |
| vocation | job |

## Writing is really rewriting

"Sceptics say that writing cannot be taught. ... Offering to teach it is a rash act. Yet something that can be taught is preparation: decent mastery of your material, orderly planning of how to set it out. Another thing that

can be taught is revision. For the writer, the great value of the written word is that it is improvable."
John Whale from *Put it in Writing*

## More editing tips

Apostrophes should be used to indicate that something belongs to or is "of" something. Grammatically speaking, these are called possessive apostrophes. Some examples: "The Iraqi people's human rights". "It is Katie's homework".

To form the possessive of a singular noun not ending in an "s" sound, add an apostrophe s. Thus: John's book.

To form the possessive of a singular noun that ends in an "s" sound, note the way the word is pronounced. If a new syllable is formed in the pronunciation of the possessive, add an apostrophe s. Thus: the witness's reply.

If the addition of an extra syllable makes a word ending in "s" difficult to pronounce, add the apostrophe only. Thus: Brahms' melodies.

For regular plural nouns (those that end in "s" or "es"), add only an apostrophe to form the plural possessive. Thus: the old boys' network.

With irregular plural nouns (those that do not end in s), add apostrophe s to form the plural possessive. Thus: women's networks or men's problems. Most of the irregular plural nouns relate to people: men, women, people, children.

**Tip**: If the possessives make the sentence feel ugly, rewrite the sentence.

Use possessive pronouns with gerunds. The sentence "I could not endure him whining about Sarah" is wrong because it is unclear whether I could not endure him or his whining. Thus you should write "I could not endure his whining about Sarah."

Be careful with their and there. Which is correct: "They had their coffee there." Or "They had there coffee their"? It's the former because their is a possessive pronoun. Always leave yourself time to proofread your article at least twice to edit and make corrections.

**A warning about word processors**
Word-processing software like Word tries to help by suggesting corrections. But sometimes the software can be wrong. By following its advice you will appear stupid. Beware of supposedly helpful software. Use your brain, not the software.

Here is a list of things to avoid in your writing.

**Clichés**: Tired phrases masquerading as literature
**Tautology**: Saying the same thing twice such as "He didn't turn up so he failed to join us.")

**Slang** (okie dokie, no worries)
**Repetition** (Mr Gray said it was a nice day. "It's a nice day today," Mr Gray said.)
**Jargon** from the police and courts (the offender, collateral damage)

**Examples of clichés**
Blazing inferno
Nipped in the bud
Breakneck speed
All walks of life
Long arm of the law
Radical transformation
Burning ambition
Cherished belief
Stick out like a sore thumb
Sweeping changes
Take the bull by the horns
Bolt from the blue
Paint a grim picture
Quick as a flash
Partner in crime

**Capitals**
Correct use of capitals is important. Best to use lower case as much as possible and employ capitals only where appropriate, such as for proper nouns (see page 9).

Appropriate use of capitals is the difference between helping your Uncle Jack off a horse and helping your uncle jack off a horse ☺

**Self-edit questions**
• Does the introduction work? Or is it dull or misleading, causing readers to expect something that does not follow?
• What is the point of the article/report? What is the writer trying to say?
• Are any words vague or abstract?
• Is everything clear and easily understood? Read aloud any parts you think are unclear. Your inner ear will detect the flaws. Re-write that section.
• Is the writing sensory? Does the article evoke any pictures in your mind? Did it make you hear or smell or feel or taste or see anything?
• Is it overburdened with clichés, dull words, plodding sentences?
• Does it have too many adjectives and adverbs?
• Do quotes from interviews sound authentic?
• Does the writing run smoothly, drawing you inexorably towards the end? Or is it disconnected, difficult to follow, or repetitive?
• Do you have to backtrack to figure out what was going on? If so, re-write.
• Is anything missing? Is there a gap that makes you say to yourself, "But what about...?"
• If the article seems too long, what is of least interest? What could be cut or condensed without weakening the argument?
• Is the grammar, spelling, punctuation and syntax so good that you never noticed any flaws? Or are you occasionally irritated or confused by things like poor punctuation?

# Chapter 7: Style

IN THE CONTEXT of writing, style has two meanings. The first relates to consistency of expression. Most publications have a "style book" to ensure that words with varied spelling like Baghdad or Bagdad are printed the same way each time they are used. It is an attempt to impose order and standardise meaning, just as the rules of spelling and grammar do the same for the English language.

All news organisations adopt a stylebook. If you write for a specific publication you will need to learn that style.

The second meaning relates to personal style. Each of us writes in a certain way based on our personality, culture and education. Authors are said to have a "voice". This term describes the unique style of an author, just as each person has a unique sound when we hear them speak. If you adopt the messages in this book you will learn the skill of writing. Plus you will also express yourself in a way that is special to you.

This chapter relates mostly to the first meaning of the word "style". Most of the suggestions here are designed to help you write more clearly and succinctly.

Most stylebooks are organised in dictionary form, and then include sections on punctuation and specialised topics. Broadcasters have their own form of stylebook because in this situation the words will be read aloud, and the style will be designed to suggest a more conversational approach.

Some of the most relevant rules found in print-based or online publications are developed here to help you write more clearly.

**Paragraphs**: Most newspapers use one paragraph per sentence, whereas essays employ longer paragraphs. If a sentence contains one idea, a paragraph contains enough sentences to develop that idea more fully.

**Past tense**: Most newspaper reportage is written in the past tense because the event has already happened by the time the piece appears, probably the next day. Most non-fiction should also be written in the past tense for the same reason.

Be consistent with **tense**: "He said she was at the meeting" not "He said she is at the meeting." Also be consistent in subject and verb agreement. A singular subject requires a singular verb, and a plural subject requires a plural verb.

**People**: Use full names on first reference. Most print publications use "Mr", "Ms" or "Miss" or other titles such as "Professor" or "Dr" plus last names for later references.

**Numerals**: Use numbers for all addresses, ages, amounts of money, dates and percentages. (Spell out "per cent.") In most other references, spell out numbers that are single digits (four, five, etc) but use digits for more than single digits (2.3, 44, 191, etc).

Spell out any number that begins a sentence. Years can be tricky, so rather than starting a sentence with a year it is best to find another approach such as rephrasing the sentence to move the number away from the start. Use the dollar sign and a decimal with specific amounts of money over 99 cents. Use commas in numbers beyond 999 (22,378); use decimals ($1.32 million) for numbers of more than 1 million, except when a specific figure is essential.

**Dates and times**: Times other than noon and midnight are given as numerals followed by am or pm. Omit trailing double zeroes (7am, not 7.00am). Do not use letters after a date, such as "May 1st or January 3rd" (better to write May 1 or January 3).

**Capitals**: Use lower case as much as possible because it makes text easier to read. If it's a common noun, use lower case. Capitalise formal names of organisations and people (these are proper nouns). Avoid acronyms and abbreviations unless they are very familiar to the reader (such as the BBC). Write the name of organisations in full at first, put the abbreviation in brackets after that first mention, and then use the abbreviation. Thus it would be the British Medical Association (BMA) and then BMA thereafter.

**Quotes**: Use double quote marks on direct quotations, with attribution. Long quotes can be broken into paragraphs, leaving off the end quote mark on the first paragraph. Use single quote marks for quotes-in-quotes.

If you use a part quote in a sentence, the double quote marks come inside the punctuation. Thus: "I'm going to have a good time in Paris," he said. But: She said that when she went to Paris she would have "a good time".

Often we can imply (and thus delete) that and who when these words are connected with the verb to be. Thus: "These are the books that are required for the course" is better expressed as "These books are required for the course."

Who/that/which: Use **who** for people, and **that** and **which** for animals and inanimate objects. Thus: "He is the person who applied for the job" not "He is the person that applied for the job."

Always use "more than" before numbers, not "over". Thus: More than 15,000 attended the concert, not Over 15,000 attended the concert. Use over when you intend to suggest movement or direction, as in "over the bridge".

Finally, never start a sentence with "There is/are/were/has/been ..." That structure is the sign of an amateur. You can always find a better way of phrasing a sentence by putting the subject at the start.

**Quotes to remember**
"Clear thinking becomes clear writing; one can't exit without the other. It's impossible for a muddy thinker to write good English."
William Zinsser, from *On Writing Well*

"Only ambitious nonentities and hearty mediocrities exhibit their rough drafts. It's like passing round samples of one's sputum."
Vladimir Nabokov, novelist

"The secret of good writing is to strip every sentence to its cleanest components. Every word that serves no function, every long word that could be a short word, every adverb that carries the same meaning that's already in the verb, every passive construction that leaves the reader unsure of who is doing what — these are the thousand and one adulterants that weaken the strength of a sentence."
William Zinsser, from *On Writing Well*

# Chapter 8: Ideas

CURIOSITY AND IMAGINATION remain a writer's most valuable assets. How do we generate ideas? By satisfying our curiosity. And then use imagination to develop those ideas.

One of the best ways to find ideas is to read widely. Monitor magazines and specialist publications as well as the web. Read letters to the editor. Look at signs in shop windows. Plus advertisements in magazines. Posters and flyers in shops. Even graffiti on walls.

Maybe you read that a man has invented a new and easy way to crack macadamias, the world's hardest nut. What are the possibilities of a story behind this man and his nutcracker? What started him on the nutcracker trail? How many years of trial and effort went into this triumph? What does he do for a living when not inventing things? What is the export potential for this gadget? And what about his other inventions?

What questions generate the best answers? Those answers might form the basis for a publishable piece.

All writers should maintain an ideas file, especially if you are going to operate as a freelance journalist or if you need new things to write about for essays. Keep clippings and print-outs in an electronic or paper file. Scan or photograph posters or notices with your mobile phone and transfer them to your file.

You hear a politician being interviewed on radio or television. She mentions her dream as a child was to become a fireman. In itself that might not mean much. But how about using your imagination? What about the childhood dreams of your local politicians? Maybe they really wanted to be professional boxers, or circus clowns, or farmers. You need to strengthen your imagination muscles to develop story ideas.

Avoid abstract concepts and think specifics. An increase in company tax will not directly affect the ordinary person in the street. But two pounds more on a bottle of wine might.

## What interests readers?
No two readers are alike but here is a list of things that interest most people. Develop your own list. Many good stories qualify under more than one heading.
- **Novelty**. Consider a familiar pattern with a new twist. Or an event that has never happened before. Nude polo players?
- **Personal** impact. The average reader is a parent, owns or rents a house, intends to buy a new car, or looks forward to a holiday. Stories about education policies, children's diseases, house prices, new schools, or cheaper cars or holidays will attract them. Stories about people like him/herself give the reader a chance to identify.

- **Money**. Fortunes made and lost. Taxes and budgets. Rent increases, wage rises or freezes, economic crises. Increases in petrol costs. This can be classified under the general term the "hip pocket nerve".
- **Sex**. It remains one of life's greatest motivating forces and is a constant pre-occupation even in societies where it is not talked about openly. Weddings of famous or infamous people. Multiple marriages and divorces. Affairs of the rich and famous.
- **Conflict** or action. Wars, strikes, explorers' discoveries, revolutions, elections and the power battle of politics. When aggression is channeled, the spectator always takes sides, even if s/he starts out neutral.
- **Religion**. Even the agnostic will read about religious reform movements, the elections of Popes – or the unfrocking of a priest.
- **Humour**. Deliberate or accidental humor can relieve to the drudgery of everyday life. Satire, silly anecdotes, jokes and cartoons are all attractive to readers.
- **Human** interest. We're all interested in our neighbours. Human happiness or ordeal will produce strong emotions. Stories of kindness, cruelty and sudden success are generally always read.
- **Underdog**. One of the great themes of literature and drama, because most of us are underdogs in some way – buffeted by the whims of our employer, our landlord, our teachers or officialdom.

- **Health**. We ask our friends when we meet them "How are you?" Health is a popular topic of conversation and reading. Things like miracle surgery, medical advice columns, famous invalids, technological advances that may prolong life.
- **Movies / TV**. Many people enjoy visiting a theatre or cinema, or watching television, because we want to be entertained. Audiences enjoy reading about the world of "show business" or "celebrities".
- **Food / drink**. Few subjects can give more pleasure or cause more anxiety. A businessman drops a million on a bottle of wine. Shortages and gluts, genetically modified crops, food poisoning scares: these are all possible topics.
- **Groups**. Every city is full of minority interests. Only a small percentage of newspaper readers may be chess players — but almost every member of this group will read the chess column.

We end as we began: If you can walk or talk, you have evidence that you can learn to write, provided you follow the techniques in this book and apply yourself. Good luck and happy writing.

Useful books about writing

- Blundell, William. *The Art and Craft of Feature Writing*. New York: Plume, 1986.
- Franklin, Jon. *Writing for Story: Craft Secrets of Dramatic Nonfiction*. New York: Plume, 1994.
- Gardner, John. *On Writers and Writing*. Boston: Addison-Wesley, 1994.
- Gardner. John. *The Art of Fiction*. New York: Vintage Books, 1985.
- Goldberg, Natalie. *Thunder and Lightening: Cracking Open the Writer's Craft*. New York: Bantam, 2000.
- Goldberg, Natalie. *Writing Down the Bones: Freeing the Writer Within*. Boston: Sambhala, 1986.
- King, Stephen. *On Writing: A Memoir of the Craft*. New York: Scribner, 2000.
- Nelson, Victoria. *On Writer's Block: A New Approach to Creativity*. Boston: Houghton Mifflin, 1993.
- Zinsser, William. *On Writing Well*. New York: Harper Resource, 2001.

## Courses and workshops

Stephen Quinn offers a range of writing **courses** and **workshops**. These could be a **one-day** workshop to sharpen your skills on a specific subject through to **weekly meetings** over two months for people who want a sustained critique of their work.

He also runs courses for people who would like to learn how to make **broadcast-quality videos** using only an iPhone. Everything from research, filming, editing, narration, captions, titles and uploading can be done from the mobile. Examples of Stephen's videos made with only an iPhone can be found at this site https://www.youtube.com/user/NingboMojo/videos

For more information, email Stephen at sraquinn@gmail.com or DM him on Twitter @sraquinn or SMS him at +44(0)793-99-70-100

## About the author

This is Stephen Quinn's 29th book. He is professor of mobile phone journalism at the Westerdals Institute for Film and Media at Kristiania University in Norway. He also runs MOJO Media Insights (MMI), a digital consulting business, based in Brighton in the United Kingdom. He mostly trains media professionals to make broadcast-quality videos using only an iOS device, usually an iPhone.

From 1996 to 2011 Dr Quinn was a journalism professor in Australia, the UAE, the US and China. Between 1975 and 1995 Dr Quinn was a journalist with Australian newspapers, the *Bangkok Post*, the UK's Press Association, BBC-TV, ITN, *The Guardian*, and TVNZ. He returned to journalism with the *South China Morning Post* in Hong Kong from 2011 until 2013 before he moved to the UK. His PhD from the University of Wollongong in Australia focused on diffusion of innovation. He writes a weekly wine column.

You can contact Stephen Quinn, and read the wine columns, at http://sraquinn.org/

# Notes

www.ingramcontent.com/pod-product-compliance
Lightning Source LLC
Chambersburg PA
CBHW062151100526
44589CB00014B/1782